DATE DUE

OCT 1 6 1998	
OCT 2 9 1998	
DEC 2 1 1998	
JAN 1 2 1999	
JAN 2 1 1999	
MAR 0 2 1999	
NOV 0 6 2000	
FEB 1 9 2003	
MAR 2 6 2003	
APR 9 2003	
JUN 1 6 2005	
JAN 6 2006	
JE 2 0 '08	
NOV 1 7 2009	

DEMCO, INC. 38-2931

FOOTBALL LEGENDS

Troy Aikman

Terry Bradshaw

Jim Brown

John Elway

Brett Favre

Michael Irvin

Vince Lombardi

John Madden

Dan Marino

Joe Montana

Joe Namath

Walter Payton

Jerry Rice

Barry Sanders

Deion Sanders

Emmitt Smith

Lawrence Taylor

Steve Young

CHELSEA HOUSE PUBLISHERS

JOHN ELWAY

Dan Hirshberg

Introduction by
Chuck Noll

CHELSEA HOUSE PUBLISHERS
Philadelphia

Produced by Daniel Bial and Associates
New York, New York

Picture research by Alan Gottlieb
Cover illustration by Bradford Brown

First Printing

1 3 5 7 9 8 6 4 2

Library of Congress Cataloging-in-Publication Data

Hirshberg, Dan.
    John Elway/Dan Hirshberg; introduction by Chuck Daly.
    p. cm. — (Football legends)
    Includes bibliographical references and index.
    Summary: Traces the football career of the quarterback for the Denver Broncos.
    ISBN 0-7910-4395-9 (hardcover)
    1. Elway, John, 1960–   —Juvenile literature. 2. Football players—United States—
Biography—Juvenile literature. 3. Denver Broncos (Football team)—Juvenile literature.
[1. Elway, John, 1960–   . 2. Football players.] I. Title. II. Series.
GV939.E48H57   1997
796.332'092—dc20
[B]   96-34789
                                                                                              CIP
                                                                                               AC

CONTENTS

A WINNING ATTITUDE

Chuck Noll

Don't ever fall into the trap of believing, "I could never do that. And I won't even try—I don't want to embarrass myself." After all, most top athletes had no idea what they could accomplish when they were young. A secret to the success of every star quarterback and sure-handed receiver is that they tried. If they had not tried, if they had not persevered, they would never have discovered how far they could go and how much they could achieve.

You can learn about trying hard and overcoming challenges by being a sports fan. Or you can take part in organized sports at any level, in any capacity. The student messenger at my high school is now president of a university. A reserve ballplayer who got very little playing time in high school now owns a very successful business. Both of them benefited by the lesson of perseverance that sports offers. The main point is that you don't have to be a Hall of Fame athlete to reap the benefits of participating in sports.

In math class, I learned that the whole is equal to the sum of its parts. But that is not always the case when you are dealing with people. Sports has taught me that the whole is either greater than or less than the sum of its parts, depending on how well the parts work together. And how the parts work together depends on how they really understand the concept of teamwork.

Most people believe that teamwork is a fifty-fifty proposition. But true teamwork is seldom, if ever, fifty-fifty. Teamwork is *whatever it takes to get the job done.* There is no time for the measurement of contributions, no time for anything but concentrating on your job.

One year, my Pittsburgh Steelers were playing the Houston

Oilers in the Astrodome late in the season, with the division championship on the line. Our offensive line was hard hit by the flu, our starting quarterback was out with an injury, and we were having difficulty making a first down. There was tremendous pressure on our defense to perform well—and they rose to the occasion. If the players on the defensive unit had been measuring their contribution against the offense's contribution, they would have given up and gone home. Instead, with a "whatever it takes" attitude, they increased their level of concentration and performance, forced turnovers, and got the ball into field goal range for our offense. Thanks to our defense's winning attitude, we came away with a victory.

Believing in doing whatever it takes to get the job done is what separates a successful person from someone who is not as successful. Nobody can give you this winning outlook; you have to develop it. And I know from experience that it can be learned and developed on the playing field.

My favorite people on the football field have always been offensive linemen and defensive backs. I say this because it takes special people to perform well in jobs in which there is little public recognition when they are doing things right but are thrust into the spotlight as soon as they make a mistake. That is exactly what happens to a lineman whose man sacks the quarterback or a defensive back who lets his receiver catch a touchdown pass. They know the importance of being part of a group that believes in teamwork and does not point fingers at one another.

Sports can be a learning situation as much as it can be fun. And that's why I say, "Get involved. Participate."

CHUCK NOLL, the Pittsburgh Steelers head coach from 1969–1991, led his team to four Super Bowl victories — the most by any coach. Widely respected as an innovator on both offense and defense, Noll was inducted into the Pro Football Hall of Fame in 1993.

1

"THE DRIVE"

It will forever be known as "The Drive."

John Elway, the Denver Broncos' star quarterback, has led many sensational fourth-quarter winning or tying drives, but none will surpass the one he mastered on January 11, 1987, in ice-cold Cleveland Stadium.

The American Football Conference (AFC) championship game pitted Elway against another young rising quarterback, Bernie Kosar of the Cleveland Browns. It was a clash of styles, with Kosar a cerebral signal-caller specializing in throwing mid-range passes from the pocket and Elway a strong-armed and fleet-footed athlete loving to scramble and throw deep. Both had storied college careers, Elway at Stanford University, Kosar at the University of Miami. Both came into the game with something to prove. And the winner of the game would go on to meet the New York Giants in Super Bowl XXI.

Using his exceptional scrambling ability, John Elway escaped a would-be tackler in the 1987 playoff game against Cleveland.

Denver got to the title game by posting a Western Division leading 11-5 record and beating the New England Patriots 22-17 in a conference semifinal playoff game. The Browns finished the regular season as the Central Division champs and as the best team in the league by virtue of their 12-4 record. They rose to the occasion late in the year, winning their last five regular season games. They advanced to the championship game by taking a thrilling double-overtime win over the New York Jets. That set the stage for Kosar and Elway, both playing in their first league championship game.

It was a brutally cold day at the stadium along Lake Erie, with the temperature at game time fixed at 20 degrees. The threat of snow made the gray skies seem even more dark and gloomy. The winds whipped violently throughout the contest, making it feel like it was just 5 degrees. Even for those who aspire to play in "real football weather," the conditions in Cleveland that day were difficult to take.

Elway knew he would have to have a perfect game in order to win because the Broncos had a weak running attack that year. Sammy Winder was Denver's leading ground-gainer with just 789 yards, averaging a mere 3.3 yards a carry. While Winder did rush for 102 yards in the win over New England, there was no reason to believe he could repeat his performance against Cleveland. Gerald Willhite was the team's second leading rusher with 365 yards with Elway, whose ability to scramble out of trouble made him that much more dangerous to opposing defenses, not far behind, with 257 yards. So the load all year fell to Elway, who threw the ball 504 times, completing 280 passes for 3,485 yards.

Kosar led a balanced attack, with a running game that featured two formidable backs. The year before, Kevin Mack and Earnest Byner each rushed for 1,000 yards—the first time teammates ever combined for that feat. Mack became the main man for the Browns in 1986 after Byner was injured in the seventh game. At the time, Byner was leading the Browns in both rushing and receiving. His return for the game against the Broncos was sure to spark the Browns' offense.

The game, played before a sellout crowd of 79,915, was a barn-burner all the way. Cleveland scored first on an opening quarter 14-play, 86-yard drive, capped by a Kosar to Herman Fontenot 6-yard pass to take a 7-0 lead. In the second quarter, Denver got on the scoreboard after Jim Ryan intercepted a Kosar pass at the Brown 9 yardline. Although the Broncos could not score a touchdown, Rich Karlis nailed a 19-yard field goal.

Denver got another break on the Browns' next play when Mack fumbled and Jim Woodard recovered for the Broncos on the Browns' 37. On first down, Elway rambled 34 yards and three plays later, it was fourth-and-goal at the one. Willhite plunged the final yard and Karlis' extra point made it 10-7. Cleveland countered with 20 seconds left in the half by getting a 29-yard field goal from Mark Moseley.

Karlis and Moseley traded field goals early in the second half, and then Cleveland took a 20-13 lead with 5:48 left in the game when Kosar hit Brian Brennan on a 48-yard touchdown pass. It looked even worse for the Broncos on the ensuing kickoff. The ball sailed to the 15 yardline and then bounded to the 2 before Gene Lang finally fell on it. Denver needed to go 98 yards in a hurry if it wanted any chance of winning.

Elway knew he had only enough time left for one drive. Ninety-eight yard drives are extremely rare—sometimes an entire season goes by without any team putting one together. To create such a drive, all while battling the clock, the weather, and a strong opponent, would be little short of a miracle. Most teams, when faced with a first down at the 2 yardline are more concerned with gaining just a few yards so their punter can kick securely, not with figuring out a way to score.

And yet, the Broncos refused to quit. As the team huddled in the endzone, All-Pro left guard Keith Bishop broke the ice, telling his teammates, "Now we've got them where we want them!"

With the wind blowing in his face, Elway brought his team to the line of scrimmage. Calling signals, he looked right, then left. Elway took the snap and quickly tossed to Winder for five yards to get the Broncos out of the immediate hole. For some coaches, a pass in such a situation would be too dangerous to try, but with Elway's quick release, a pass made as much sense as a run. Winder ran the next two plays and picked up a first down. Elway next ran for 11 yards, then completed passes to Steve Sewell and Steve Watson, bringing the Broncos to the Brown 40.

Elway's next pass fell incomplete. He dropped back to pass again, and was sacked for an 8-yard loss. Now the season was truly on the line. Dan Reeves, the Broncos coach, would have been happy if the team could have gotten just a 10-yard gain, allowing them a reasonable chance to pick up the remaining eight yards on a fourth-

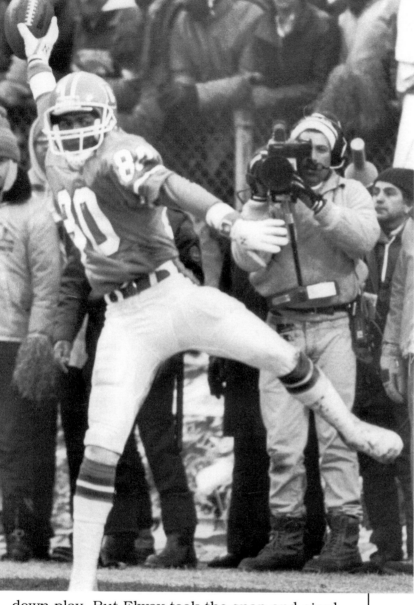

Mark Jackson holds the ball high after he scores the tying touchdown on an Elway pass in the fourth quarter of the 1987 AFC title game.

down play. But Elway took the snap and aired out a long pass to Mark Jackson. Jackson caught it for a 20-yard gain and a first down.

"Their safeties were playing real deep and Mark did a great job of finding the hole for me. I just put the ball up there," related Elway after the game.

Two plays later he hit Sewell again and the Broncos were still alive at the 14 yardline. Only

57 seconds remained in the game. Elway threw incomplete, then dashed nine yards to the 5 yardline. On the next play, Elway capped the improbable drive by completing a touchdown pass to Jackson. Karlis's extra point tied the game with 39 seconds left in regulation, stunning the Brown's crowd, especially those sitting in the famed Dawg Pound, where zealous fans dressed up as dogs and barked and yelped throughout the game.

Mike Horan, the Bronco punter, remembers the drive well. "I kept thinking, `just keep getting first downs, keep driving the ball.' I kept praying that the drive would keep going. And it seemed like everytime it was third-and-long somebody would come through. The one great thing about playing for John is that you know you've always got a shot."

In overtime, only the second in playoff history (the first was in 1962 when the Dallas Texans beat the Houston Oilers), the Browns won the coin toss, but Denver's defense held tight and Cleveland was forced to punt. Elway took his team at the 25 yardline and engineered another terrific drive. He worked the Broncos upfield using both the run and short passes. The Broncos got to midfield and faced a third and 12 when Elway hit a wide-open Steve Watson in the center of the field for 28 yards and a first down. Winder then ran the ball three straight times to the 15 and seconds later, Karlis drilled a field goal for the 23-20 victory.

"We really had the momentum going [into overtime]," said Elway. "I didn't mind that they had won the coin toss. I knew our defense would stop them. They did, we got the ball and made a couple of big plays."

While the overtime drive was a good one, it was the fourth-quarter drive that will be remembered forever. For Elway, it was the greatest of many fourth-quarter comeback drives he'd had already and had yet to come. He completed 6 of 9 passes for 78 yards and rushed for another 20.

"It was the greatest drive I've ever been involved with," Elway said. "We just had to dig down and find out what we were made of. Everybody on the line gave me plenty of time to throw and the receivers got open. We just came out fighting and clawing and got the job done."

In the end, Elway accounted for 300 of his team's 374 total yards, rushing for 56 yards and passing for 244.

"We worked on containing Elway all week and we did until the very end," Cleveland coach Marty Schottenheimer said dejectedly after the game. "He's a great player who makes the plays that win championships."

"They had us backed up most of the afternoon," Reeves added. "But whenever you have a John Elway as your quarterback, you've got a chance."

John Elway was born on June 28, 1960, in Port Angeles, a tiny town in western Washington. He led his way into the world moments ahead of his twin sister, Jana. Jack and Janet Elway were already the parents of a daughter, Lee Ann.

Football runs in the Elway family. John's grandfather, Harry Elway, was a quarterback; he once played against the Carlisle Indians and the legendary Jim Thorpe. Jack Elway played quarterback at Washington State University, and then became a coach. Jack had already coached at the University of Montana and at the time of John's birth, he was an assistant football coach at Washington State.

John started to play organized football in sixth grade, joining a team in Missoula, Montana, called the Little Grizzlies. Initially, he was a running back and did a pretty good job of moving the ball. Over time, John developed a very strong arm, telling people later on that he'd throw any-

As a teenager, John Elway was a great baseball and basketball player as well as a football player.

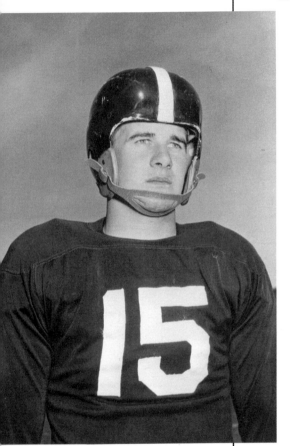

John Elway's father, Jack, played quarterback for the Cougars of Washington State University.

thing from dirt clods, snowballs and stones, and throw at all sorts of targets. "I'd set up bottles on a fence and knock them down all day long," he had said.

In junior high school, Elway made the transition from running back to quarterback and by the time he was ready for high school, it was obvious that he could throw the ball as well as, if not better, than anyone around.

In 1976, Jack Elway was hired as the head coach at California State University at Northridge. Realizing his son had some serious talent, Jack wanted to make sure that he attended a high school that could take advantage of his skills.

Granada Hills High School, located outside of Los Angeles, not only had a reputation as a winning football program, it also was well known for its passing game. Head coach Jack Neumier incorporated a complicated, wide-open, quick-passing offense that not only won him laurels from other coaches, but championships as well. Yet while Jack Elway had all the confidence in the world in his son, John still had to prove himself at Granada Hills.

"I didn't know much about him," recalls Neumier, who regularly called for 40 passes a game. "He came in as a 10th grader and had to learn our system, which was very hard."

"When he moved in nobody knew who this guy was," says Daryl Stroh, who was an assistant football coach under Neumier and later replaced him as the head coach. "He didn't start for a couple of weeks but it became real obvious soon that he was a real talent."

Elway spent the first few weeks as the junior varsity quarterback, learning the system and showing the coaching staff what he could do. By mid-season, he had made his impression. With the varsity struggling, Neumier brought the sophomore up to the first team.

"We weren't doing too well," says Neumier. "Then we brought him up and we started winning right away. He went on to have a fine year and we made the playoffs."

Elway had three terrific years at Granada Hills, completing 60 percent of his passes for 5,711 yards and 49 touchdowns. He took his team to the league championship and to the state semifinal game. His senior year was cut short by a knee injury, yet he still managed to complete 129 of 200 passes for 1,837 yards and 19 touchdowns.

"He went down in the fifth game," remembers Neumier like it was yesterday. "He was doing super."

Elway recovered in time to play in the annual spring North-South high school shrine game his senior year and promptly "broke every record imaginable," according to Neumier. If anyone in the region didn't know about Elway by then, they understood his capabilities full well by the end of the contest."

"He always had a great arm," says Stroh. "But his greatest asset was his competitiveness. He loves to be there when it's on the line. It's always been like that. And he is a real hard worker. I'd just enjoy watching him play. I still enjoy watching him on TV. What was real nice was that he was always upbeat. He was always glad to be there whether it was practice or a game. I never saw him having a bad day."

Today, his teammates talk of his leadership ability. That quality started in high school. "He was a quiet leader," assesses Stroh of Elway, who had his number 11 uniform retired by the school. "He wasn't very vocal. He wasn't loud or boisterous or demanding. He was very well liked and people naturally followed him. He really led by doing."

"And in the process, learned his lessons well. "Fundamentally he learned a lot in high school," says Neumier. "We would go over a 10-minute drill everyday. No huddle, no stoppage. Just see how many plays we could get in. We also used a lot of audibles in our system. All that toughened him mentally."

Elway won the school's prestigious Thom McAn Trophy for most outstanding scholar/athlete in his senior year. "They were starting to recruit him then," Neumier said. "Everybody wanted him. I knew he was going to be good in college." In high school, Elway weighed about 175 pounds. His coaches saw he was still growing and could carry 200 or more pounds by the time he reached the pros.

There were some who felt Elway could also be a pro in baseball. Elway, who was a fine basketball player as well, had three excellent years at Granada Hills as an outfielder, third baseman, and pitcher. Football and a college education, however, were Elway's priorities his senior year. He was the most sought-after high school football player in the country in 1979 and had been named by a host of magazines, including *Parade, Scholastic Coach* and *Football News*, to their All-America teams. The recruiters came from all over, from the east, from the south, from the midwest and even more close to home. In the end, it boiled down to a handful of choices. The University of Southern California, Stanford University, the University of Missouri, Notre Dame and San Jose State, where his father now coached, were all in the running.

Finally, Elway chose Stanford. Stanford had the best academic reputation of all these schools, and although its football team did not have the greatest winning tradition, John had been a fan of the Pac-10 since his childhood. A big factor in Elway's decision was the Cardinals' history of turning out professional quarterbacks. Many people refer to the college as the "quarterback school." Over the years, the school has produced future NFL signal-callers such as John Brodie, Jim Plunkett, Frankie Albert, Gary Kerkorian, Bobby Garrett, Dick Norman, Dave Lewis, Mike Boryla, Don Bunce, Guy Benjamin, Steve Dils, and Turk Schonert. All graduated from Stanford to the pros and Elway had dreams of joining the exclusive group.

Jack Elway coached many fine quarterbacks on his college teams—but he had no better student than his son, John.

3

RECORD-BREAKING CARDINAL

During the four years John Elway spent at Stanford, the Cardinals never were able to field a top-flight team. Stanford's football team lost more games than it won and the Cardinals were not invited to play in any bowl games. And yet, the fans all had reason to be hopeful and excited before each game. John Elway provided thrills each time he took a snap and dropped back to pass. As a freshman, Elway was not a frequent starter, although he saw plenty of action in his freshman year. He completed 50 of 97 passes for 544 yards, with 6 touchdowns. After the season, Paul Wiggin was brought in as head coach, replacing Rod Dowhower.

Elway became the full-time starter in his sophomore year. A highlight of the season came in the third game when Elway led the Cardinals to a convincing 31-14 upset over the University of Oklahoma. But the Cardinals sagged later in

John Elway had his choice of colleges to attend. He chose Stanford University because it had a tradition of turning out pro quarterbacks.

the season and finished with a 6-5 record. Elway completed 248 of 379 passes (a terrific 65 percent average), for 2,889 yards, and 27 touchdowns. The 248 completions broke former Cardinal Steve Dils' Pac-10 season record of 247, set in 1978. Elway also broke the league mark for total offense, amassing 2,939 yards, breaking another Cardinal's record, Jim Plunkett's 2,898 yards set in 1970. Additionally, Elway passed for 4 fourth-quarter touchdowns against Oregon State, and this tied an NCAA mark.

Elway was recognized for his outstanding season, becoming the first sophomore quarterback in 18 years to be named to an All-American team (*The Sporting News*) and was tapped the Pac-10's Player of the Year, the first time a second-year player was given such an honor.

While his junior year was somewhat of a disappointment after he suffered an ankle injury, Elway still produced some terrific numbers. He completed 214 of 366 passes (58 percent) for 2,674 yards, and 20 touchdowns. It was a rough year for the team, though, which finished a lackluster 4-7.

Coach Wiggin, who had spent 23 years in the National Football League as a coach and All-Pro player and is currently the Director of Pro Personnel for the Minnesota Vikings, was impressed with his quarterback, not only for his football skills, but for his other endeavors, both in school and out.

"John was raised right," the coach says of Elway. "He could keep a B average, even when he was taking a lot of classes. And he'd always find time to do things like visit the local children's hospital."

When he was on the football field, he was at his best, though. And his senior year was one of

the greatest seasons ever posted by a quarterback. He broke his own league record for completions, connecting on 262 out of 402 attempts, for 3,242 yards, the latter two marks also shattering the Pac-10 record previously held by Dils (391 attempts and 2,943 yards in 1978).

In one incredible game, Elway broke the Pac-10 record for most attempts in a game, throwing the ball 62 times against Ohio State University. In that game, played on September 25 in front of 89,436 Buckeye fans, Elway rallied the Cardinals from a 13-0 deficit by completing 22 of 36 passes for 284 yards in the second half, including a game-winning 18-yard touchdown strike to Emile Harry with just 34 seconds left in the game for a final score of 23-20. Elway fin-

The Stanford Cardinals had few fine players while Elway played there. Here Elway is sacked by Bob Metheny of the San Jose State Spartans as he fails to find an open receiver downfield.

ished the nationally-televised contest with 35 completions for 407 yards and 2 touchdowns.

Elway also engineered road victories over Purdue, 35-14, Washington State, 31-26, and led an awesome attack that upended No. 1 Washington, 43-31. Against Washington, Elway ripped open the Huskies' vaunted defense for 265 yards and 2 touchdowns on 20 of 30 passing. At one point, he completed 12 straight passes as Stanford scored 30 consecutive points to change a 17-7 deficit into a 37-17 lead. Elway finished the game with a flourish, completing 16 of 17 passes.

Although Stanford had again had a losing record, this time going 5-6, the good-looking Elway's heroics had become legendary. His ability to make things happen drew praise from everywhere, as the voting for the Heisman Trophy —the most famous college football award— loomed.

"He has a super quarterback mind," says Wiggin, discussing the Elway of yesterday in much the same way he discusses the Elway of today. "He can see so much more than any other quarterback. If one guy is not open, he can go to the number two receiver and if he's covered, he can still go to number three. He's got natural instincts, is a great scrambler, makes great reads, and has a great arm. The arm is incredible and puts him over the top. But what makes him so special is his quarterback mind. You're not born with that."

"I consider Elway to be the best quarterback in history, at this level, anyway," said Purdue head coach Leon Burtnett. "John knows when to roll out of the pocket and when to step into it. There isn't anyone who can stop him. Elway just throws the ball so hard, our linebackers couldn't react. They almost stood flat-footed. He's got my [Heisman] vote."

"John Elway is the best quarterback I have ever seen in college football," declared Joe Avezzano, Oregon State's head coach. "I can't see how anyone else at this time can get the Heisman Trophy away from him, unless the Eastern press keeps it at home. I'll be damned if anybody else is better than Elway. Without Elway, Stanford is a completely different team. With him, they can win against any team."

"There's probably never been anyone who's had a greater impact on the game of college football than John Elway," added Arizona State head coach Darryl Rodgers. "He may be the best quarterback in the history of the NCAA."

In addition to starring at football and baseball, Elway also carried a full academic load at Stanford, graduating with a degree in economics.

Elway's numbers were concrete evidence of his greatness. He finished his illustrious college career by completing 774 of 1,243 passes for 9,349 yards and 77 touchdowns, setting nearly two dozen Pac-10 and NCAA records in the process. These records included: most completions in a career, most seasons gaining 2,500 or more total offensive yards, and most games gaining 200 passing yards or more in a career. In addition, his pinpoint passing yielded interceptions in just 3.13 percent of his total pass attempts. In the Pac-10, he set new standards for career passing yards, pass attempts, completions, touchdown passes, and total offense.

"And he did it in the framework of different systems," points out Wiggin. "He adapted to every offense he was shown and he did it well. This is a guy, don't forget, who had to carry more of the load than most quarterbacks in the game. If you look at his career, from the pros on down, that's the way it's been."

But despite all his credentials, Elway came in second in the Heisman voting. Herschel Walker, a junior running back at the University of Georgia won and running back Eric Dickerson came in third.

Elway would not have to live with disappointment long. The NFL draft was coming up, and those in the know were calling him the consensus number one pick. By now Elway stood 6'3" and weighed a strong 215 pounds. "John Elway is the best quarterback prospect I've ever seen," said Dick Steinberg, the New England Patriots Personnel Director. "He is the best player in college football today. He has no flaws."

"He's probably the best college quarterback I've ever seen," agreed San Francisco 49ers coach Bill Walsh. "He's big and mobile, reads defenses very well, and in the system at Stanford, which is quite complicated, he is the man who makes it work."

In his final collegiate football game, Elway got to play for his father for the first time. Jack Elway, the San Jose State coach, was selected to head the West team in the annual East-West Shrine game. The younger Elway, who had played against his father four times in college (Stanford won the first two, San Jose the next two), responded in typical fashion. He was named the game's most valuable offensive player.

At the end of 1983, Elway graduated Stanford with a degree in economics and a solid B average. A pro football career beckoned. Or did it?

Football was John Elway's main sport through high school and college, but it wasn't the only one. He also played basketball and baseball. His basketball career was cut short in his senior high school year after he suffered a knee injury in football, but his baseball career continued in earnest. A line-drive hitter, Elway batted .551 his junior year and .491 his senior year, helping Granada Hills win Los Angeles city championships in 1978 and 1979.

"He was just a great player," says Daryl Stroh, the team's coach. "He had great instincts and had an outstanding arm."

Elway played right field in his sophomore and junior years, then moved to third base as a senior. Batting third in the lineup, Elway also pitched, going 4-2 in his senior season. As a left-handed batter, Elway didn't have much power, yet he regularly sprayed the ball to all fields. In his last two seasons, in fact, he was held hitless in just one game.

In Elway's last two years at Granada Hills, his team won city championship games at Dodger

At Stanford, Elway showed grace in the field and a strong arm—when he played baseball as well as football.

Stadium. The 1978 title game was truly memorable for Granada Hills. Elway started at third base in the game against Crenshaw High School and its dominant outfielder, future major leaguer Darryl Strawberry. Hills got out to an early lead, but Crenshaw started putting runs on the board and cut into that lead. Elway had not pitched in six weeks, but Stroh asked him to take the mound. Elway allowed Crenshaw only one hit over the last five innings. Elway was credited with the victory as Granada Hills won, 10-4.

The Kansas City Royals were impressed by Elway's baseball talents. Although he had already signed his letter-of-intent to attend Stanford, the Royals drafted Elway in the 18th round, hoping he would prefer a pro baseball career. (The year before, Kansas City used this strategy to draft Willie Wilson, who had broken nearly every New Jersey state record for running backs. Wilson went on to a distinguished career as a baseball player.)

"There was no doubt in my mind that he could make it [in the pros]," said Stroh. "He did so many things well. With that cannon of an arm he could have played shortstop. It was amazing how good he was in everything he did. And even though he didn't have a curveball—he didn't have a great pitch in that respect—he could throw heat."

Elway turned down the Royals, but he continued to play baseball at Stanford. As a freshman, he hit .269 in 46 games, stealing 8 bases, banging 3 doubles, 2 triples and 1 homer. His hitting improved dramatically in his sophomore year, his average rising to .361 (in 49 games), with 15 doubles, 1 triple and 9 homers. As an outfielder (and occasional relief pitcher), he drove

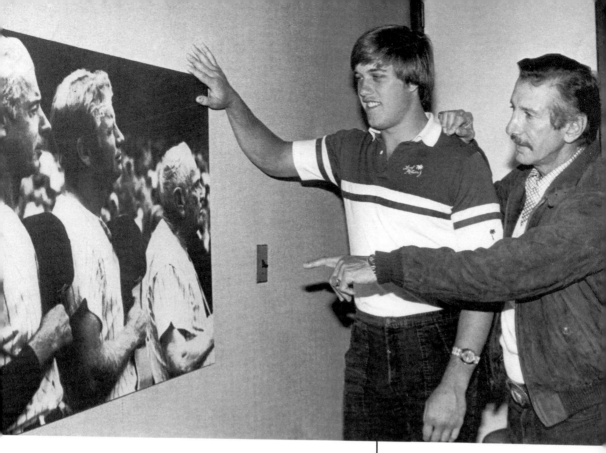

in 50 runs and scored 47. In the NCAA Central Regionals, Elway was selected to the all-tournament team after whacking the ball at a .444 clip. All this while going to spring football drills.

"If John played nine months of the year, instead of three or four, there's no telling how good he could be," Stanford baseball coach Mark Marquess said.

George Steinbrenner, owner of the New York Yankees, was enamored with Elway and his team selected the Stanford star in the first round of the 1981 draft. The Yankees offered Elway a $140,000 contract to play for their Oneonta farm club that summer and he accepted, even though that meant he would no longer be eligible to play college baseball by NCAA rules. The Oneonta Yankees are located in rural upstate New York

George Steinbrenner, owner of the N.Y. Yankees, thought Elway had a great future in baseball. After Elway's stint with the Oneonta Yankees was over, Steinbrenner invited John to his office, where Yankee manager Billy Martin pointed out a picture of Yankee greats Joe DiMaggio, Mickey Mantle, and Casey Stengel.

and play in the New York-Penn League, which has a short summer schedule. Most of the teams are made up of former college players, a rung up from players signed right out of high school. The season had already started before Elway arrived and his stint there lasted only six weeks.

It was a big media attraction, of course, with ESPN and other networks trekking up to Oneonta for an "exclusive." Newspapers and magazines, not just from the New York area, were up there in droves, too. Elway was the biggest story in normally quiet Oneonta.

"Oneonta is like a lot of little teams in the [New York-Penn] league," remembers Ken Berry, the former Chicago White Sox player who managed the team that summer. "The fan support is the same no matter what. As for John, he was a real class kid. He fit right in with the other kids. He walked to the park—he didn't have a car. He never played the role that he was the number one quarterback at Stanford or that he was bigger than someone else because he got a lot of money to play a short time. The media tried to make it bigger. *Sports Illustrated, The Sporting News*, ESPN, Los Angeles, somebody was always calling. They were always inquiring about him. I tried screening some of it, but it did get pretty hectic at times."

Elway got off to a sluggish start. Once he got comfortable though, he started stinging the ball. He finished with a .318 batting average and knocked in a team-high 24 runs. He played exclusively in the outfield and made no errors. When Elway graduated from Stanford less than two years later, the Yankees made a bid to sign him again.

"We feel Elway could be a star in New York," said Steinbrenner. "We think it would take him another three years in the minor leagues, but that would be good for him. He wouldn't be in a pressure situation right away."

Though Steinbrenner and his aides were high on Elway, Berry wasn't completely sold. "I was sure he could make it as an outfielder [in the majors], but I wasn't so sure he would be an all-star," said Berry, now a minor league hitting instructor with the New York Mets. "He might have been a quality fourth outfielder, but he wasn't the kind of guy who hit for a lot of power and he didn't have a lot of speed. Until he learned the ins and outs of hitting, he probably would have hit in the .260-.270 range with eight to ten homers a year. Really, he was better suited for football. And the more I watched him on TV, the more I was convinced that football was the route he should take."

While Elway used the baseball alternative as an option following the NFL's college draft in the spring of 1983, it was more of a veiled threat. Football, all along, was his route of choice.

4
NUMBER 1

The NFL Draft held on April 26, 1983, was one of the most unusual ever. Never before or since has one draft featured so many outstanding college quarterbacks. By the end of the first round, a record six signal-callers had been picked, with Penn State's Todd Blackledge going to Kansas City, Pittsburgh's Dan Marino heading to Miami, Illinois's Tony Eason bound for New England, Ken O'Brien of the University of California at Davis heading to the New York Jets, and the University of Miami's Jim Kelly being picked by Buffalo. The last time an NFL draft had drawn as many as four quarterbacks in the first round was in 1954.

All five of these other quarterbacks chosen in the first round of the 1983 draft became starters for their respective teams (although Jim Kelly played for a number of years in the fledgling United States Football League before joining the

On draft day, 1983, the Baltimore Colts had to decide if they wanted to pick Elway even though he had already said he did not want to play for the team.

35

Al Harris of the Chicago Bears grabs hold of John Elway, who has no way to escape. Elway—who was sacked nine times in this game—had a tough rookie year in the NFL.

Bills). Each had at least a respectable career; in fact, all but O'Brien and Blackledge got to play in the Super Bowl.

Which one of these great quarterbacks would be picked first? The Baltimore Colts, thanks to their 0-8-1 record the previous year, had the first pick in the draft, and head coach Frank Kush declared that John Elway was his man.

Elway wasn't thrilled with the possibility of playing for the Colts, and voiced his opinion several times before the draft was held. He felt the team lacked a solid offensive game plan. In addition, his father had come to dislike Kush; the two had faced off against one another when Kush was the head coach at Arizona State. The Colts did entertain some pre-draft offers, but in the end, they chose Elway with their first pick. Hours later, Elway told the Colts that they'd made a big mistake, that he'd never play for them. Jack Elway told reporters point blank that John "will never play for (Colts owner Robert) Irsay or Coach Kush."

For several days the two parties were at an impasse. To make matters more difficult for the Colts, the Yankees were reportedly dangling a big money contract at Elway and he played that card in a big way. "Right now it looks like I'll be playing baseball with the Yankees," he said to reporters. "It will be a couple of days, or maybe even two weeks before I make the final decision. We haven't ruled out football, but it doesn't look good right now." In addition, the Elway family talked with officials from the USFL and Canadian Football League.

After a week, Irsay finally acknowledged that signing Elway would never happen. On May 2, he concluded a deal with Denver Bronco owner Edgar Kaiser, Jr. Denver sent Baltimore offensive guard Chris Hinton, its first-round pick in the 1983 draft, quarterback Mark Herrmann, and its first-round pick in 1984.

Elway was ecstatic. "I'm definitely thrilled to be here," he said. "It's something I didn't expect to happen. I'm glad to be playing in the NFL and I'm glad to be playing for the Denver Broncos." Irsay, bitter over being rejected, bad-mouthed Elway following the trade. "He will never be any good in the NFL," Irsay grumbled.

Elway's edict to the Baltimore Colts would haunt him for some time, though. Some members of the media, other players, and even fans got on his case, referring to him as a "brat" and a "crybaby" because he demanded to be traded. Of course, some of these people may have been jealous of the contract the Broncos offered Elway: $5 million dollar for five years. This made him the highest paid player in the NFL—and he had yet to throw his first pass!

Elway announced that spring that he was going to get married in 1984 to fellow Stanford senior Janet Buchan, his girlfriend since his freshman year. Buchan had been quite an athlete as well, setting a host of American and World Games swimming records.

Denver was coming off a disappointing year in 1982. In fact, it was a disappointing year for the league. The season, cut short by a strike, saw the Broncos finishing the campaign at 2-7.

The pre-season hype on Elway was immense. By the time Elway got to the team's University of Northern Colorado complex, it was blanketed by hundreds of members of the media, many of whom were declaring the Broncos a Super Bowl contender because of their new star. The pressure was on and the start of the season was still weeks away.

Toward the end of the training camp, coach Dan Reeves announced that Elway would be Denver's starting quarterback on opening day. The early going was rough for Elway, though, whose pro debut was an inauspicious one as he completed just 1 attempt in 8 passes against the Pittsburgh Steelers. It didn't get that much better in the next few weeks. The jump from college to the pros was a tough one. He had difficulty reading NFL defenses and keeping pace with the fast style of the pros. "I've got a long way to go and I have a lot to learn," Elway said to author Dennis Eichhorn. "It just takes experience. Pro players are much better and faster than college players. It's going to take me a while to get used to that."

After five games, Reeves decided that Elway needed a break from the pressure and gave the starting quarterback job to Steve DeBerg. Under the veteran, the Broncos clicked and reeled off four straight wins. But then DeBerg separated a shoulder and was lost for several weeks. Elway was back in charge. The break apparently helped the rookie. Although he still took his lumps, Elway started to show signs that he was made for the NFL. In one game, he completed 16 of 24 passes for 284 yards and 2 touchdowns to spark a victory over Cleveland. In an emotionally charged game against Baltimore, the team Elway had spurned, Denver won a tight game when John completed 23 of 44 passes and threw 3 fourth-quarter touchdowns to win, 21-19.

Even after Elway was sacked four times by the New York Jets, Coach Dan Reeves expressed confidence in his quarterback.

The victory put the Broncos into the playoffs with a 9-7 record, and much of Denver's improvement can be credited to the arrival of Elway. Still, in the first-round wild-card playoff game against Seattle, Reeves opted to go with DeBerg as the starter. The Seahawks were hot that day, though, and jumped out to a big lead. Elway came in late in the game and completed 10 of 15 passes for 123 yards, but it was too late. The Seahawks won, 31-7.

In the off-season, the Broncos showed how much confidence they had in Elway by trading DeBerg to the Tampa Bay Buccaneers. They picked up Scott Brunner from the New York Giants, but clearly his role would be to back up Elway.

Elway responded by putting up stellar numbers. In 1984, he completed 214 of 380 passes for 2,598 yards, with 18 touchdowns and 15 interceptions. At times he was brilliant, including the game against Minnesota when he tied a club record by firing 5 touchdown passes in a 42-21 win, the team's 10th in a row, which also set a new team record.

During this season Elway showed the NFL what kind of dangerous quarterback he could be. He could run, throw off the wrong foot, or throw across his body. Analysts agreed he had the strongest arm of any quarterback in the game. He was also the best scrambler. As a lefty, he gave fits to defenses normally used to chasing righthanded quarterbacks. He knew how to give himself maximum time to find a receiver open downfield. If everyone was covered, that usually meant he had some running room in front of him. John would take off for the first-down marker, and if that meant taking a vicious hit, so be it. Elway's strength sometimes meant that tacklers got the worst of any collision. Opponents learned that Elway was at his most dangerous when the play the Broncos called had broken down and their star quarterback had to start improvising.

Elway finished the season as the Broncos' third-leading rusher with 237 yards. Denver won 12 of the 14 games he started (a knee injury sidelined him for two games). The Broncos' 13-3 record was the best in team history. But Denver again was knocked out of the playoffs in the first round. The Broncos were leading 17-10 in the third quarter, but the Pittsburgh offense scored two touchdowns to take the lead and its defense stopped Denver twice late in the game to seal a 24-17 victory.

While Elway had a fine season, it was not all smooth sailing. He made sophomore mistakes and the fans sometimes booed his performance. Perhaps more alarming is that he and Coach Reeves occasionally argued on the sidelines during games, many times about play selection. Their relationship, in fact, remained rocky until Reeves was let go at the end of the 1992 season.

Elway's first child, Jessica, was born October 17, 1985, and in celebration he rewrote the Denver record books. He set single season marks for attempts (605, which led the NFL and fell just four short of Dan Fouts's NFL-record 609), completions (327, second in the NFL), passing yards (3,891, second in the NFL), total rushing and passing plays (656, first in the NFL), and total offense (4,414, first in the NFL). In all, he completed 54 percent of his passes, and in a win against Seattle, threw for 432 yards. He also rushed for 253 yards and a 5.0 average carry. But for Denver, the season ended in disappointment. Despite going 11-5, the Broncos did not make the playoffs. Yet the table had been set. In the next four years, Denver would make it to the Super Bowl three times.

QUARTERBACK SNEAKS.

5
SUPER YEARS

The Denver Broncos were charter members of the American Football League in 1960, but it wasn't until the latter part of the 1970s, when they had long since been merged with the NFL, that the Broncos became consistently successful. Under Coach Red Miller, the Broncos reached the Super Bowl in 1977, when they lost to the Dallas Cowboys. In the ensuing years, more often than not, Denver won many more games than it lost. Yet it would take nine years for the Broncos to make it to a conference title game again, let alone a Super Bowl.

In 1981, Dan Reeves, the one-time Cowboy running back, replaced Red Miller as coach. Beginning with the 1986 season, and lasting four glorious years, Reeves would lead the Broncos to some of the greatest of times and some of the most frustrating of times.

Two years before their Super Bowl matchup, John Elway posed with Joe Montana in a sneaker commercial.

Lawrence Taylor (56) and Leonard Marshall (70) of the New York Giants celebrate a sack of Elway during the 1987 Super Bowl.

In 1986, the Broncos had become a solid veteran ball club with Elway as their leader. Denver's fans certainly expected the best and for the 17th straight year they bought out every available ticket for every home game. The Broncos whipped through their first five opponents. When they beat San Diego, 31-14, to stretch their record to 6-0, they were off to their best start ever. Denver slumped a bit down the stretch, but still finished 11-5 and won the AFC West. During the season, 35 individual and team records bit the dust.

Defensively, Denver was very strong, with defensive end Rulon Jones and linebacker Karl Mecklenburg leading the way. On offense, Elway was still the mainstay, and the team had given him some fleet receivers to work with. Although statistically he did not have his best year, Elway had several outstanding games and made the Pro Bowl for the first time. For the second straight year he threw for over 3,000 yards. In addition to the 19 touchdown passes he threw, Elway caught one himself. His 23-yard TD reception from Steve Sewell remains an NFL record for full-time quarterbacks.

In late December, with a Mile High Stadium record crowd of 76,105 watching in delight, the Broncos stopped the New England Patriots, 22-

17. The Patriots took a 17-13 lead midway in the third quarter, but Denver came back on its next possession, going 86 yards in six plays, with Elway hitting Vance Johnson for 48 yards for a touchdown on the last play of the quarter. Rulon Jones's sack of Patriot quarterback Tony Eason in the endzone supplied the Broncos with the final margin of victory.

The win over New England set up the game against Cleveland and perhaps the greatest drive in NFL history, Elway's 98-yard fourth-quarter drive to tie the Browns. In overtime, Elway engineered another long drive to clinch the victory and set up a meeting with the New York Giants in Super Bowl XXI.

All season long, the fans were on Elway's side, and his heroics against Cleveland seemed to cement a positive relationship forevermore between the quarterback and the fans. Never was it more evident than at a January 18 Super Bowl rally at Mile High Stadium when over 63,000 fans gave Elway and the Broncos a banner send-off.

The Giants, who featured the NFL's best defense in 1986 and had not given up a touchdown in two playoff games, feared Elway. All-Pro linebacker Lawrence Taylor suggested, "The biggest thing we have to do is to take care of John Elway. We have a lot of respect for him." In fact, the Giants got a mouthful of Elway during the regular season. His best game of the season statistically came in November in a game against the Giants when he completed 29 of 47 passes for 336 yards and rushed for 51 more, though New York won, 19-16.

During the first half of the Super Bowl, Elway was in his prime. On the first play from scrimmage, Elway ran for 10 yards. He completed his first six throws and hit on eight of ten to give Denver a 10-9 half-time lead. But in the second half, the Giants hit the big plays. Their defense stiffened and with quarterback Phil Simms completing 22 of 25 passes for 3 touchdowns, New York emerged with a 39-20 decision. Elway finished with 22 completions in 37 attempts for 304 yards and 1 touchdown and led the Broncos in rushing with 27 yards, including a 4-yard touchdown run in the first quarter. "I felt I did everything I could," said Elway. "I gave 110 percent. That's all I could do."

As disappointed as Elway and his teammates were, they were not totally shaken. After all, they felt that they were a young team and that they'd only begun to make waves. The only problem, as the 1987 season unfolded, nobody was sure whether or not the NFL season would take place. Even as the Broncos were losing an August pre-season game, 28-27, to the Los Angeles Rams in American Bowl '87 in Wembley Stadium, England, the football headlines were about labor problems, not about wins and losses. The season did get underway — but not for long — as Denver split its first two games. A players' strike was called on September 22. After a week's worth of games were cancelled, the owners decided to use replacement players. For three weeks, until a contract was finally ratified, replacement teams were fielded by every NFL team. The Broncos' replacement players won one game out of three, and so, when the regular squads began play nearly a month later, Denver was struggling to get to .500 and its high hopes were suddenly strained. But later in the season, the Colorado team caught fire. They won four in a row, and six of their last seven games, finishing the year at 10-4-1 and winning the western division crown. The Broncos, playing in a blizzard in Denver, clinched the title December 27 when they shut out San Diego, 24-0. It marked the team's third AFC title in four years and was the club's eighth 10-win season since 1977.

Voted the Broncos' offensive MVP, Elway had four 300-yard passing games that year, setting a new club mark, and he led all NFL quarterbacks in rushing for the fourth consecutive season, gaining a career-high 304 yards, ranking him second on the team.

In the playoffs, Denver crushed the Houston Oilers, 34-10, and held on to knock off Cleveland for the second straight year in the AFC title game, 38-33. This set up a showdown with the Washington Redskins in Super Bowl XXII. Many people thought that it would be a close game, with oddsmakers giving the small but quick Denver team an edge of 3½ points, mainly because of Elway and three receivers in particular: Vance Johnson, Mark Jackson, and rookie Ricky Nattiel, a group affectionately known as the Three Amigos.

Washington featured a big, strong team, and were led by Doug Williams, the first black quarterback to play in the Super Bowl. As it turned out, Williams, who was relatively unheralded, emerged as the center of attention and the game

Dave Butz of the Washington Redskins puts pressure on Elway during Super Bowl XXII.

was anything but close in warm and sunny San Diego. Less than two minutes into the game, Elway threw a 56-yard scoring strike to Nattiel that set a Super Bowl record for earliest touchdown scored. But that was virtually Denver's only moment of glory. The Redskins erased a first quarter 10-0 deficit and pummeled the Broncos, 42-10. Williams was named the MVP after completing 18 of 29 passes for 340 yards and 4 touchdowns. To add insult to injury, little known rookie running back Timmy Smith tore through Denver's defense, racking up 204 yards on the ground. Elway completed just 14 of 38 passes for 257 yards, However, he was intercepted an uncharacteristic three times. He did catch a pass, a 23-yarder from Steve Sewell.

At the completion of the season, Elway, now the father of two daughters (Jordan Marie was born in June), was showered with awards and honors, from AP's Most Valuable NFL Player to *The Football News*'s AFC Player of the Year. Still, the Super Bowl loss could not make up for the awards and honors. The loss to Washington left a bitter taste in his mouth.

In the off-season, the Broncos got a player they thought would make the Super Bowl difference for them. In June, they acquired future Hall of Famer Tony Dorsett from the Dallas Cowboys. And while Dorsett did move into second place on the all-time rushing list behind Walter Payton in September, it would be a rough year for both the Broncos and Elway. Denver finished with an 8–8 record and did not make the playoffs. Elway, who suffered from a variety of nagging injuries throughout the season (he missed one game after spraining his ankle), still put up some fine numbers. His 3,309 passing yards and

234 rushing yards made him the first NFL player in history to eclipse 3,000 passing yards and 200 rushing yards in four straight years.

The 1989 season brought back better times for Elway and the Broncos. On November 26th, Denver took a 38-0 halftime lead en route to a 41-14 thrashing of Seattle clinching its third AFC title in four years. Elway, in scintillating fashion, threw for 217 yards and 4 touchdowns in the first half. In the divisional playoff game against Pittsburgh, he was 12 of 20 for 239 yards, and rushed for 44 yards, to lead an exciting come-from-behind 24-23 victory. In what was becoming more commonplace each season, Elway engineered another fourth-quarter game-winning drive. Behind all game, the Broncos got the ball at their own 29 yardline with 7:06 left. After

John Elway enjoyed his best postseason game in the 1990 AFC championship against the Cleveland Browns. Unfortunately, two weeks later the Broncos lost their third Super Bowl in four years, as they were crushed by the San Francisco 49ers.

a nine-yard gain, Elway handed the ball to running back Bobby Humphrey who pitched it back to Elway; John then heaved a pass to Vance Johnson for 36 yards and a first down at the Steeler 26. The Broncos went to the ground game the rest of the drive with fullback Mel Bratton bursting through for the final yard with 2:27 to go. David Treadwell's extra point kick gave the Broncos the victory.

"He (Elway) is so exciting," says linebacker Michael Brooks, who played with Denver from 1987-92. "You always knew that if you were behind, he had the ability to bring you back in the game. It was amazing how many games we won in the fourth quarter. When the game is on the line, he's probably the best in the game to have in there."

By the time the Broncos got to the fourth quarter in its AFC title game a week later against Cleveland, in Denver on a fall-like afternoon, they didn't need any comeback drives. Indeed, within minutes of the fourth quarter, Denver was in complete control, leading 31-21. Two late field goals made it a 37-21 final and for the third time in four years, Denver was the AFC champion (all three times beating Cleveland in the title game). Elway had a terrific game, throwing for 385 yards and three touchdowns, including a 70-yarder to Michael Young. He also rushed for a team-leading 39 yards. As a team, the Broncos piled up 497 yards of offense. Yet it was Elway's ability to make things happen that was the difference. All game long Elway eluded the Browns' rush, improvising as necessary, buying time when no time existed, and making a play when absolutely none was available.

"He's deadly," offers wide receiver Arthur Marshall, who played with Elway from 1992-93. "Especially when he gets out of the pocket. I felt more comfortable when he had to scramble out of the pocket. When he gets out of the pocket anything can happen. He might run for 10 yards or he might throw a 60-yard pass downfield that's on the money. It's unbelievable."

Following the win over Cleveland, Coach Reeves simply said, "If there is any question as to how great an athlete John Elway is, he showed everyone today. Elway never quits."

And Elway wasn't about to quit as he faced his third opportunity in four years to win a Super Bowl game. This time, Elway, now a 29-year-old veteran, would be taking on the powerful San Francisco 49ers at the Superdome in New Orleans. But it was another frustrating evening for Elway and the Broncos. The loss to Washington ended up seeming tame because this Super Bowl game would truly be an embarrassment for Denver. San Francisco clobbered the Broncos, 55-10, as Joe Montana completed 22 of 29 passes for 297 yards. Before you could bat an eye, the NFC champs led 13-3 and by halftime, it was 27-3. Elway completed only one of his first 10 passes, and the second completion did not come until the 27th minute of the game. By then, San Francisco led 20-3. Super Bowl parties around the country barely lasted into the second half, if that long.

In four years, the Broncos lost three Super Bowls. They would not get a chance to get revenge soon.

6

HALL OF FAME MATERIAL

Even though the Denver Broncos lost big-time to the San Francisco 49ers in Super Bowl XXIV optimism still reigned in Colorado. After all, the Broncos still showcased one of the NFL's best teams. However, since losing to San Francisco, the Broncos have made the playoffs only twice, making it all the way to the AFC championship game in the 1991 season before losing to Buffalo and getting knocked out of post-season play in a wild card game in 1993 against the Los Angeles Raiders. During that time, there have been three coaches in Denver—Dan Reeves, Wade Phillips, and Mike Shanahan. Many players have come and gone. One of the few constants during this time span has been quarterback John Elway, whose hobble-like swagger and unconventional actions on the field have already made him legendary.

The 1990 season was particularly disappointing for Broncos fans. Denver never recov-

Elway plays with his daughter Jessica during practice.

ered from a six-game losing streak and finished with a 5-11 record, one of only two times in Elway's tenure that the team failed to win at least half its games. There were few highlights for the club in 1990. Bobby Humphrey rushed for 1,202 yards and Mike Horan led the NFL in punting, the latter note usually going hand-in-hand with a losing team. Ironically, Elway completed 294 of 502 passes for a completion percentage of .586, the highest of his career. He also threw for 3,526 yards and 15 touchdowns, and rushed for 258 yards, piling up a career-high 52 in one game against the Raiders.

In 1991, the team's fortunes dramatically changed for the better. The team that some people said was getting old and heading nowhere resurfaced to win the AFC West with a 12-4 mark. It started with the Broncos' biggest opening day win, a 45-14 decision over Cincinnati. Elway, now the father of four (Juliana was born that March; a son, Jack, was now two years old), had perhaps his best opening-day game ever, throwing for 262 yards and 2 touchdowns, catching a 24-yard pass, and scoring 2 TDs on the ground. In early December, the Broncos clinched their fifth divisional title in eight years. If that wasn't enough, that old Elway fourth-quarter magic act returned in a huge way in the playoffs against Houston. Just as the 1986 AFC championship game will forever be known as "The Drive," the 1991 divisional game against the Oilers will be remembered as "The Drive II." Down 21-6 in the second quarter, the Broncos chiselled away at the lead, yet still trailed 21-16 at the end of the third quarter as a sellout crowd of 75,301 fans at Mile High Stadium shifted nervously in their seats.

Early in the fourth quarter, Al Del Greco's 25-yard field goal made it 24-16. But the Broncos battled back, and sparked by a do-or-die fourth down 26-yard completion by Elway to Michael Young, they were still alive. Three plays later, Greg Lewis scored his second touchdown of the game from one yard out and now Denver was down by just one point.

The Oilers failed to move the ball as time ticked away, but a punt left the Broncos hovering at their own 2 and things looked dim as 2:07 showed on the clock. What's worse, Denver had no timeouts left. However, Elway, showed he still knew how to engineer a memorable drive. He hit Young for 22 yards on first down before the Broncos. Three more plays netted only four yards. Facing a fourth-and-six, Elway dropped back to pass. Everybody was covered, so he scrambled seven yards for a first down. The next three passes fell incomplete, though, and again the Broncos faced another fourth down and long. Elway dropped back to pass; he started to run upfield, but before crossing the scrimmage line, he tossed a pass to Vance Johnson who ran to the Oiler 21. Three plays and 10 yards later, David Treadwell whacked a 28-yard field goal for the victory as time elapsed. Afterwards, coach Reeves commented, "I'm numb, that's the biggest way to describe it. To overcome what we overcame was amazing. But when you got No. 7, anything is possible."

Elway, comparing this win from the Cleveland win, said, "Against Cleveland we had three timeouts but had to score a touchdown. Here, we had no timeouts and only had to score a field goal. I couldn't really feel the difference. There was the same amount of pressure and they were

*Even in his 30s, Elway
showed he could still run
as well as throw, as he made
Trace Armstrong of the
Chicago Bears miss a tackle.*

both great." Years later, Mike Horan recalled that "it was big. The Oilers were really taunting us after they scored to make it 24-16. They kept saying that we weren't going to come back this time, no way. But right way, after that lob pass to Johnson we knew there was a chance."

Unfortunately, the Broncos couldn't carry the momentum the next week and they were stopped by the Buffalo Bills, 10-7, in the AFC title game at Rich Stadium. It was expected to be a shoot-out between the Elway-led Broncos and the Jim Kelly-led high-powered no-huddle Bills, but instead turned into a defensive struggle. It was

0-0 at the half before Buffalo tallied a third-quarter field goal and an early fourth-quarter touchdown to take a 10-0 lead. And while the Broncos did counter with a last-quarter TD, there would be no chance for a heroic fourth-quarter drive by Elway because he sustained a thigh injury at the end of the third quarter and was replaced by Gary Kubiak.

Things were looking pretty good early on for the Broncos in 1992, as they won seven of their first 10 games. But disaster struck when Elway bruised his right shoulder against the New York Giants. The injury sidelined the star quarterback for four weeks and not coincidentally, the Broncos lost four in a row. Elway returned in the 15th week and the Broncos split their last two games, finishing 8-8 but falling short of a playoff spot. At the end of the season, Dan Reeves, whose welcome had been worn in Colorado, was let go after accumulating a 116-78-1 record. On January 25, 1993, Wade Phillips was hired to replace him. Elway responded to the change by recording his best season. At age 33, he completed a league-leading 348 of 551 pass attempts for 4,030 yards and 25 touchdowns. His 63.2 completion percentage was a personal high and also led the circuit. More important to Elway was that while the Broncos did not win the western division title, they did make the playoffs as a wild card team as a result of their 9-7 record.

The contest against the Raiders at the Coliseum, turned out to be a shootout-deluxe, at least for a half. Knotted at intermission, 21-21, Los Angeles exploded in the second half, outscoring the visitors 21-3 for a 42-24 decision and sending the Broncos home wondering what went wrong. Elway had a terrific first half and finished with 29 completions in 47 attempts for 302 yards and 3 touchdowns. In the second half, though, Denver's offense sputtered while the Raiders' offense continued to seemingly score every time they had the ball.

The 1994 campaign proved to be a difficult one for both Elway and the Broncos, who slipped to 7-9. Elway missed a pair of games late in the season because of a knee sprain and the Broncos lost both outings. In addition, he was sacked 46 times, a career high for him and a figure that led the entire NFL. Following the season, the Broncos made another coaching change, replacing Phillips who had come into disfavor with the Denver contingency with former Bronco assistant coach Mike Shanahan signing a seven-year deal. Shanahan, who had been the offensive coordinator with San Francisco for the previous three years, was prepared to take the Denver offense to new heights.

In many respects, he did do that. One of his first acts was to hire Gary Kubiak as the quarterback's coach. With Shanahan and Kubiak in his corner for 1995, Elway was excited. And even though he was now 35, he started all 16 Bronco games and complemented by rookie Terrell Davis's 1,117 rushing yards, proved just as dangerous as ever. He completed 316 of 542 passes for 3,970 yards (58.3 percent) with a career-high 26 touchdowns. Showing that he's still not afraid to run with the ball he gained 176 yards on 41 carries, a 4.3 average pick-up.

In November, he surpassed 40,000 yards passing for his career (on the same day that Warren Moon turned the trick), thus joining Fran Tarkenton, Dan Marino, Dan Fouts, Joe Montana, and

Johnny Unitas in that exclusive club. Midway through the year, as the Broncos tried to stay in playoff contention, there was no denying that its offense was one of the best. "This offense gets better and better every week," said Elway. "The offensive line and the talent we have at the skill positions really make us tough. You look forward to what you can do on offense."

Consecutive losses late in the year to Seattle and Kansas City, though, all but ended Denver's chances for a playoff spot, the first time the Elway-led Broncos would go two straight years without making the playoffs. In the season finale, as rumors began to swirl about whether or not Elway would return in 1996, Elway did pull one last magic act, bringing the Broncos from behind in the fourth quarter to beat the archrival Raiders, knocking them out of the playoffs in the process. It was Elway's 37th career fourth quarter game-winning or game-saving drive, an unofficial league record. During the course of the season, the 13-year veteran moved into fifth place in the all-time completion list, went over the 3,000 yard passing mark for the 10th time, joining Marino as the only one to do it, moved into third place on the all-time NFL list for total offense and third in pass attempts. Twice he was named the AFC Offensive Player of the Week (13th time in his career) and he has now started more games as a Bronco than anyone else. Clearly, when you talk about the Broncos you are talking about John Elway.

"It was great for me to work with a guy like that," says Tommy Maddox, who at one time was being groomed as Elway's successor in Denver. "He is one of the best in the game. It always impressed me how hard he worked at it and how competitive he is. He is real focused on what he has to do to get it done. It may not be the way it's supposed to get done, but he gets it done somehow. When I came in (1992) some people were wondering whether he'd hang it up soon. But in the last few years, his career has taken a jump-start. He's playing as well as he ever has."

"It was great fun for me just being on the same team with him," says former Bronco kicker Brad Daluiso. "I grew up watching him on TV and it was a real pleasure to play with him."

"He is a one of a kind player," adds another former Bronco, linebacker Mike Croel. "He is a real leader. When he's around, you feel his presence."

"He is definitely the leader on the field," agrees Horan. "He's Hall of Fame material and he's got the numbers to prove it."

Curiously, none of the great quarterbacks drafted in the famed Class of 1983 won a Super Bowl game. Jim Kelly lost four with the Bills, Elway lost three, Dan Marino and Tony Eason lost one each. Still, these losses should have no effect on Marino's and Elway's chances of making the Hall of Fame.

Ah yes, the Hall of Fame. The Canton, Ohio, home of illustrious quarterbacks Joe Namath, Bart Starr, Roger Staubach, Fran Tarkenton, Len Dawson, Terry Bradshaw, Y.A. Tittle, Johnny Unitas, Norm Van Brocklin, Bob Waterfield, George Blanda, Otto Graham, Dan Fouts, Sonny Jurgensen, Sammy Baugh, Bob Griese, Arnie Herber, Bobby Layne, Ace Parker, and Sid Luckman. And some day, one John Elway? You bet.

STATISTICS

ar	G	PASSING								RUSHING			
		ATT	COMP	PCT	YDS	TD	INT	RTG		ATT	YDS	AVG	TD
83	11	259	123	47.5	1,663	7	14	54.9		28	146	5.2	1
84	15	380	214	56.3	2,598	18	15	76.8		56	237	4.2	1
85	16	**605**	327	54.0	3,891	22	23	70.0		51	253	5.0	0
86	16	504	280	55.6	3,485	19	13	79.0		52	257	4.9	1
87	12	410	224	54.6	3,198	19	12	83.4		66	304	4.6	4
88	15	496	274	55.2	3,309	17	19	71.3		54	234	4.3	1
89	15	416	223	53.6	3,051	18	18	73.7		48	244	5.1	3
90	16	502	294	58.6	3,526	15	14	78.5		50	258	5.2	3
91	16	451	242	53.7	3,253	13	12	68.3		55	255	4.6	6
92	12	316	174	55.1	2,242	10	17	65.7		34	94	2.8	2
93	16	551	**348**	**63.2**	4,030	25	10	92.8		44	153	3.5	0
94	14	494	307	62.1	3,490	16	10	85.7		58	235	4.1	4
95	16	542	316	58.3	3,970	26	14	86.3		41	176	4.3	4
TALS	190	5,926	3,346	58.5	41,706	225	191	77.8		637	2848	4.5	27

ld indicates league-leading figures

	games
T	attempts
MP	completions
T	percent
S	yards
	touchdowns
T	interceptions
G	rating
G	average

JOHN ELWAY
A CHRONOLOGY

1960   John Elway born on June 28.

1979   Drafted by Kansas City Royals but opts to attend Stanford University.

1981   Drafted by New York Yankees.

1982   Plays baseball for Yankee Single-A farm team Oneonta and leads team in RBIs.

1983   Graduates from Stanford University, is first selection in NFL draft by the Baltimore Colts who trade Elway to the Denver Broncos. Helps lead Denver to a wild-card playoff game.

1984   Leads Denver to their first western division title under his guidance. Starts first playoff game, a 24-17 loss to the Pittsburgh Steelers.

1985   Breaks several Bronco team records, including most pass attempts, completions, passing yards, and total offense.

1987   Elway engineers 98-yard TD drive in final minutes to tie the Cleveland Browns and then leads winning field-goal drive in overtime as Denver wins the AFC title. Plays in first Super Bowl game, losing to New York Giants, 39-20. Makes the Pro Bowl for the first time.

1988   Broncos lose to Washington Redskins, 42-10, in the Super Bowl but Elway is named NFL MVP.

1990   Leads Denver to third AFC crown in four years. In Super Bowl XXIV, Denver is crushed by the San Francisco 49ers, 55-10.

1992   Engineers another 98-yard game-winning drive, this one against the Houston Oilers, in a divisional playoff game won by Denver, 26-24.

1993   Elway sets personal and team season records in total offense, passing yards, touchdown passes, and completion percentage. Named AFC Player of the Year.

1995   Passes for more than 3,000 yards for the 10th time. Engineers 37th career game-winning or game-saving fourth-quarter drive in season final against Oakland Raiders.

SUGGESTIONS FOR FURTHER READING

Anderson, T.J. *John Elway.* Crestwood, 1988.

Brenner, Richard J. *Elway and Kosar.* Lynx Books, 1986.

Denver Broncos Football, Denver: Bighorn Book Sellers, 1993

Hessian, Joseph, and Michael Spence, *Broncos: Three Decades of Football,* San Francisco: Foghorn Press, 1987

ABOUT THE AUTHOR

Dan Hirshberg lives in Hackettstown, N.J., with his wife, Susan, and two children, Nathan and Melanie. He is the Executive Editor of North Jersey Newspapers in Hackettstown. He has written two previous books, *Phil Rizzuto, A Yankee Tradition,* and for Chelsea House's Football Legends series, *Emmitt Smith.*

INDEX